YOUR PLATFORM TO QUALITY TRAINING SOLUTIONS

The Ultimate Guide (1 -4)
25 Prep Questions for
NEBOSH GC 2 Exam

Copyright © 2014-2024 Raj Singh and Simply Safety Pte Ltd.

Cover page © Raj Singh and Simply Safety Pte Ltd.
Raj Singh and Simply Safety Pte Ltd. (Singapore). All rights reserved.

This book contains proprietary content and must not be duplicated, distributed, or trained from without written permission. No portion of this material may be shared or reproduced in any manner under any circumstance whatsoever without advance written permission from Raj Singh and Simply Safety Pte Ltd.
(Singapore).

First Edition: December 2014

1. What is the difference between acute and chronic health effects?

2. What are possible chronic health risks from exposure to asbestos?

3. Where will asbestos be found within the building?

4. What are control measures that should be considered before the removal of asbestos?

5. What are the ergonomic factors that could increase the risk of musculoskeletal disorders at work?

6. What are the types of object that could fall and hit a person below, when work is carried out at height?

7. What are the precautions that could reduce the risk of falling objects when work is carried out at height?

8. What are the factors to consider when reviewing the fire risk assessment after substantial changes have been made to an office building?

9. What are the precautions that may be required in order that portable electrical equipment is suitable for the location and environment in which it is used?

10. What are the possible workplace circumstances where a worker could be exposed to blood borne viruses?

11. What are the precautions that will reduce the risks from exposure to blood-borne viruses?

12. What are the control measures that can be taken to provide protection for workers who are exposed to ultraviolet radiation from sunlight?

13. What are the control measures that can be taken to provide protection for workers who are exposed to cold temperature when required to work outdoors?

14. What are the factors that should be considered when assessing the risk of a road traffic incident while driving at work?

15. What are the precautions that should be included in a safe system of work on a 230V electrical circuit?

16. What are the factors that should be considered in the manual handling assessment prior to the installation of a conveyor system?

17. What are the hazards that could be introduced following the installation of a conveyor system?

18. What are the specific risks associated with the use of a bench-top grinder?

19. What are the precautions that are required to prevent injury when using a bench-top grinder?

20. What is the meaning of the term 'work-related upper limb disorder' (WRULD)?

21. Why an office worker is at risk of developing a WRULD?

22. What are the ill-health effects that can be associated with WRULDs?

23. What are the appropriate control measures that could reduce the risk of WRULDs amongst checkout operators?

24. What is the significance of fire triangle?

25. What are three methods of heat transfer?

The Ultimate Guide 2
Another 25 Prep Questions
for NEBOSH GC 2 Exams

Copyright © 2014-2024 Raj Singh and Simply Safety Pte Ltd.

Cover page © Raj Singh and Simply Safety Pte Ltd.
Raj Singh and Simply Safety Pte Ltd. (Singapore). All rights reserved.

This book contains proprietary content and must not be duplicated, distributed, or trained from without written permission. No portion of this material may be shared or reproduced in any manner under any circumstance whatsoever without advance written permission from Raj Singh and Simply Safety Pte Ltd.
(Singapore).

First Edition: December 2014

1. What are the factors that should be considered for the safe use of a mobile tower scaffold?

2. How could fires be caused electrically?

3. What are the differences between ionising and non-ionising radiation?

4. What are two types of ionising radiation and give an occupational source for each case?

5. What are four types of non-ionising radiation and give an occupational source for each case?

6. What are the factors that may lead to a pedestrian being hit by a moving vehicle in a Workplace?

7. What are the precautions that will reduce the risks from exposure to blood-borne viruses?

8. What are the ways in which people can be injured by vehicles in the workplace?

9. What are the ways in which a vehicle driver, who is not competent, may put the safety of people in the workplace at risk?

10. What are the topics that should be included in a training programme for vehicle drivers in order to reduce the risk of accidents to themselves and other people?

11. What are the considerations to be taken when selecting a guard or safety device for piece of work equipment?

12. What are the examples of occupations that could cause WRULDs?

13. What are the possible causes of WRULDs?

14. What is the meaning of the term irritant?

15. What is the meaning of the term carcinogenic.

16. What are the ways in which the health of workers in a paint factory be monitored?

17. What are the ways that fires could be caused by electricity?

18. What is the meaning of the term Frequency?

19. What is the meaning of the term Decibel?

20. What is the meaning of the term A-Weighting?

21. What are the types of noise measurement techniques?

22. What are the hazards associated with demolition work?

23. What are the control measures to be taken when doing demolition work?

24. What are the specific types of injury that may be caused by the incorrect manual handling of loads?

25. What are the factors in relation to the load that will affect the risk of injury?

The Ultimate Guide 3
Another 25 Prep Questions
for NEBOSH GC2 Exams

Copyright © 2014-2024 Raj Singh and Simply Safety Pte Ltd.

Cover page © Raj Singh and Simply Safety Pte Ltd.

Raj Singh and Simply Safety Pte Ltd. (Singapore). All rights reserved.

This book contains proprietary content and must not be duplicated, distributed, or trained from without written permission. No portion of this material may be shared or reproduced in any manner under any circumstance whatsoever without advance written permission from Raj Singh and Simply Safety Pte Ltd.
(Singapore).

First Edition: December 2014

1. What is the meaning of the term 'work-related violence'?

2. What are the conditions where Blood Borne viruses may be present?

3. What are the conditions where Legionella may be present?

4. What are the control measures that should be taken in order to reduce the risk of accidents associated with the routine maintenance of machinery?

5. What are five hazards associated with the use of a bench top grinder?

6. What are the control measures that could be introduced to reduce risk to a worker using a bench top grinder?

7. What are the measures to be taken to minimise pollution from waste?

8. What are the advantages and disadvantages of interlocking guards and trip devices?

9. What are the ill health effects caused by vibrating tools?

10. What are the typical symptoms that might be shown by affected individuals using vibrating hand held tools?

11. What are the control measures that may be used to minimise the risk of ill health from use of vibrating hand held tools?

12. What are the factors that should be addressed in the fire plan?

13. What are THREE forms of biological agents?

14. What are the THREE possible routes of entry into the body for a biological agent?

15. What are the control measures to reduce the risk of exposure to a biological agent?

16. What is the meaning of the term acute?

17. What is the meaning of the term chronic?

18. What are the acute effects of inhalation when working with solvents?

19. What are the chronic effects of inhalation when working with solvents?

20. What are the precautions that could be taken to minimise and reduce exposure to solvents?

21. What are the effects observed on the human body after suffering from a severe electric shock?

22. What are the factors that affect the severity of injury resulting from contact with electricity?

23. What are the advantages and disadvantages of using stain tube detectors and continual gas samplers?

24. What are the control measures to prevent slip and trip hazards in an engineering workshop?

25. What are the control measures to prevent slip and trip hazards in a pantry?

The Ultimate Guide 4
Another 25 Prep Questions
for NEBOSH GC 2 Exams

Copyright © 2014-2024 Raj Singh and Simply Safety Pte Ltd.

Cover page © Raj Singh and Simply Safety Pte Ltd.
Raj Singh and Simply Safety Pte Ltd. (Singapore). All rights reserved.

This book contains proprietary content and must not be duplicated, distributed, or trained from without written permission. No portion of this material may be shared or reproduced in any manner under any circumstance whatsoever without advance written permission from Raj Singh and Simply Safety Pte Ltd.
(Singapore).

First Edition: December 2014

1. What are the control measures to be implemented when welding work is to be done?

2. What are the welfare and work environment requirements that should be provided in a workplace?

3. What are the types of injury that the worker could suffer while manually lifting boxes and placing them on shelves?

4. What are the factors that could increase the likelihood of injury when doing manual lifting?

5. What are the causes of a scaffold collapse?

6. What are the causes of a mobile scaffold collapse?

7. What are the precautions to be carried out when working on a mobile scaffold?

8. What are the precautions to be taken to minimise the risks to workers when working on a scaffold?

9. What are the items to be inspected on a scaffold?

10. What are the factors that would determine the frequency of the inspection and testing of hand held electrical equipment?

11. What is the meaning of the term 'workplace exposure limit'?

12. What are the possible reasons for increase in work related health issues for workers using solvents for which there are exposure limits?

13. What are the precautions a worker should take while using a wood chisel?

14. What are the measures to ensure the safe evacuation of persons from a building in the event of fire?

15. What are the possible hazards that rescue workers can be exposed to while attending emergencies?

16. What are mechanical hazards associated with the use of a pedestal drill?

17. What are control measures to reduce the risk of injury to operators of pedestal drill?

18. What are the factors to be considered when undertaking a manual handling assessment of the work undertaken by airport baggage handlers?

19. What are the control measures that can reduce the risk of violence between workers?

20. What are the control measures to minimise the risk of forklift trucks overturning?

21. What are the hazards of a battery powered forklift truck used in warehouses?

22. What are the precautions to be used to reduce the risk to pedestrians in the areas where the forklift trucks operate?

23. What are the steps to be taken when leaving forklift trucks unattended during a driver's work break?

24. What are the control measures to reduce the risk of injury from electricity when using a portable electrical appliance on a construction site?

25. What are the common causes of fires in the workplace?

www.ingramcontent.com/pod-product-compliance
Lightning Source LLC
Chambersburg PA
CBHW042342150426

43196CB00001B/22